Dr. Ian McDonald
www.cmbchiro.com/dr-ian-mcdonald

Dr. Bligh
www.drblighmd.com

Bone Chiro, Dr. Mary & Dr. Anna
(314) 961-1807

Pure Plates
www.pureplatesstl.com

Ofallon Nutrition
www.ofallonnutrition.com

Foxhole Partners
www.foxholepartners.wordpress.com/

Farmer Girl Meats
www.farmergirlmeats.com

I couldn't do what I do in my business without a great team to assist me, my clients and staff.

I would also like to thank Dr. Ian McDonald, Dr. Bligh, Dr. Mary & Dr. Anna of Bone Chrio, Pure Plates, Ofallon Nutrition, Foxhole Partners and Farmer Girl Meats.

Thank you Roger Semsch for all that you do for our clients, our trainers and us personally. You are a blessing to us.

Thank you to my family. My beautiful daughter Sophie who tells people I'm the healthiest woman in the world. I hope you always see me that way and I hope I encourage you to want to be the same way. To John for daily being my Superman and always keeping me fighting the good fight. My angel Molly who gave me a safe place to land for so many years. Now you bless me from heaven. To Cannon, the greatest pal a girl could ever ask for. Thanks for never leaving my side.

Introduction

I wanted to compile the best of both worlds, clean eating and inspiration. I like to think of the quotes as inspiring stories of triumph. Each picture represents a victory. Every client has a different story. Each trainer has their own history. They didn't quit  when it was difficult. They didn't stop when the motivation ran out. They changed their behavior. They learned how to become disciplined. I've heard it said that "discipline equals freedom." I believe this. We don't win the battle when the scale reads what we want or when we get taken off the medicine. We win the battle when our mind accepts that living healthy requires hard work and a lifetime of dedication. It won't be easy. It will be worth it.

These recipes are easy and best of all they taste good. You can still enjoy your food while eating clean. Even in a hyper restricted diet like mine I still enjoy these tasty meals. Your health is built by your fork and what you decide to consume daily. You cannot expect to eat terrible and feel good. I also hear a lot about moderation. I'm not in agreement with it. Balance is so important people say. What are they actually balancing? Moderation of poison is still poison. You can kill yourself slowly or quickly. Your choice. Balance is an excuse for why you still want to take in poison. I've sat in the ICU next to my father who they assumed would die. I sat next to my business associate when they said there was no way he would be ok. I've sat next to my dearest friend when they told me this is very serious you need to understand it doesn't look good. What does balance get you? When you are faced with serious consequences to your actions balance and moderation mean nothing.

There is a healthy way to get through your day. Yes it could take 30 more minutes a week. Later in life that 30 minutes could be the reason your family gets to have a second chance with you. Remove the idea that a bar for breakfast, banana for snack, and sandwich for lunch are going to leave you feeling your best each day. You need to start focusing on whole food, less ingredients, and evenly distributed nutrients.

I hope these recipes will bless you with good health. I pray that you will serve God with your body and the choices you make to keep the body he gave you healthy. Your life is a series of choices. Good and bad. If you've made mistakes with your food you are one good choice away from a clean meal. God bless you as you live a clean healthy lifestyle. Remember nothing tastes as good as being healthy feels.

Food is Fuel.

www.integritytraininggroup.com

Fitspiration

Apple Cider Vinaigrette

1/4 cup Apple Cider Vinegar
1 Garlic clove, minced
1/2 tsp. of Onion Powder
1/2 tbsp. of Stevia in the Raw
1 tsp. Spicy Brown Mustard
1/3 cup of Olive Oil

Whisk together first 4 ingredients, add oil in a slow steady stream, whisking constantly until smooth.
Add salt and pepper to taste.
Makes about 2/3 cup.

"I CAN DO ALL THINGS THROUGH CHRIST WHO STRENGTHENS ME"

PHILIPPIANS 4:13

Fitspiration

Avocado Chicken Salad

2 - 3 Boneless, Skinless Chicken Breasts
2 Avocados (peeled, pitted & mashed)
1 Chopped Celery Stick
2 tbsp Chopped Cilantro
1 Lime
Hot Sauce

Cook chicken in crock pot, shred after cooking. Add mashed avocado, celery & cilantro. Squeeze lime juice and add zest. Top with your favorite hot sauce to taste.

Recipe provided by Lisa Klaus

INTEGRITY
TRAINING SYSTEMS

JUST
ONE
MORE

Fitspiration

Baked Oatmeal with Apples

2 cups Gluten Free Oats
2 Egg Whites
1/3 cup Baking Stevia
1 tbsp Agave
1/2 tbsp Cinnamon
1 tsp Alcohol Free Vanilla
1 1/2 cup Unsweetened Almond Milk
1 tbsp melted Coconut Oil
1/2 Apple
1/4 cup Chopped Walnuts

Combine all ingredients and add to an 8x8 or loaf pan that you have lightly greased with coconut oil. Bake for 20 to 25 minutes on 350.

Fitspiration

BBQ Shredded Chicken
Served with Green Beans & Baked Sweet Potatoes

10 - 12 Boneless Skinless Chicken Breasts
2 jars Bone Sucking Sauce
Large Crock Pot

Rinse and place chicken breast in large crock pot. Pour entire jar of Bone Sucking BBQ sauce over chicken evenly. Cook on low for 10-12 hours. I prefer 12 hours. Drain chicken well. Place in a 13" x 9" pan. Use two forks and shred the chicken well. Pour the 2nd jar of Bone Sucking sauce over the chicken and stir well. Serve with baked green beans and baked sweet potatoes.

Baked Green Beans
6 bags "Steam In The Bag Green Beans"
7 tbsp Olive Oil
1 tsp Sea Salt
1/2 tsp Pepper

Microwave all 6 bags per bags instructions. Foil line a sheet cake pan. Spread green beans and combine with olive oil, salt and pepper. Bake on 350 for 30 to 45 minutes per desired doneness. Makes enough for the week.

Blueberry Egg White Pancakes

1 packet Plain Gluten Free Oats
1/2 cup of Blueberries (I prefer thawed/frozen with it's own juice)
6 Organic Egg Whites
1 tsp. Cinnamon
1 tbsp. Granulated Baking Stevia
1 tsp. Alcohol Free Vanilla (Whole Foods)
1 tbsp. Coconut Oil

Mix all ingredients in blender. Spray nonstick skillet with olive oil. Pour in skillet and cook on low to medium heat slowly until one side is done and top half is near complete. Flip and cook 2 more minutes. Spread coconut oil over the top while warm so it melts.

CONFIDENCE IS SOMETHING YOU CREATE WITHIN YOURSELF BY BELIEVING IN WHO YOU ARE.

INTEGRITY
TRAINING + SYSTEMS

Fitspiration

Bone Broth

Approximately 6 lbs Soup Bones, cut 1"-2" thick
4-6 Carrots
4-6 Stalks Celery
4 Cloves Garlic
2 tbs. Apple Cider vinegar
1 Large Onion

Brush bones with olive oil. Place on foil lined backing pan in single layer. Roast at 450 deg. for 30 minutes then turn over and roast an additional 30 minutes until bones are a deep brown. Place bones in crock pot with veggies. Put in enough water to cover bones by 1/2". Set crock pot on low and cook for 24 hours until broth is a golden brown. Remove meat, bones and veggies. Pour broth through a strainer into a large pot. This removes the food bits remaining. Place broth in fridge for 24 hours until fat sets up skip solidified fat off and dispose of it. If the broth is congealed, simply warm until liquefied then place in jars for storing. Broth will keep in fridge for 5-7 days.

Submitted by Lisa Klaus-Ogden

YOUR FUTURE IS CREATED BY WHAT YOU DO TODAY. NOT TOMORROW.

Fitspiration

Buttery Garlic Herb Chicken with Zucchini

3 tablespoons Butter
4 Garlic Cloves, minced
¼ cup freshly chopped Oregano
1 teaspoon fresh Rosemary, chopped
1 teaspoon fresh Thyme, chopped
1 pound boneless skinless Chicken Thighs, or Breasts
Salt and Pepper
2 medium sized Zucchini, sliced

In a medium sized skillet over medium high heat add the butter until melted. Add the garlic, oregano, rosemary and thyme. Add the chicken and cook for 3-4 minutes on each side or until chicken is no longer pink and 165 degrees. Remove chicken and set aside on plate. Add the zucchini to the pan and salt and pepper. Saute for 2-3 minutes or until tender. Add chicken back to the pan for a minute or so and serve. Combine all sauce ingredients and cook until thickened. Pour over the top of cooked meatloaf. Add extra herbs from meatloaf to the top.

A RIVER CUTS
THROUGH
ROCK, NOT
BECAUSE OF
IT'S POWER,
BUT BECAUSE
OF IT'S
PERSISTENCE.

Fitspiration

Cauliflower

2 bags frozen Rice Cauliflower
2 cups chopped Organic Mushrooms (any variety)
2 Shallots
1 tbsp Olive Oil
1 stick Kerry Gold Garlic & Herb Butter
1/2 tbsp Sea Salt
1 1/2 tsp Pepper
1/2 tbsp Frank's Hot Sauce

Microwave cauliflower for 10 minutes. Saute shallots and mushrooms in olive oil until soft in a large Dutch oven. Add cauliflower and cook on medium until lightly browned and fully cooked through. Add remaining ingredients to season.

EVERY MISTAKE YOU MAKE IS PROGRESS

Fitspiration

Cauliflower Stuffing

4 tbsp. Butter
1 Onion, chopped
2 large Carrots, peeled and chopped
2 Celery stalks, chopped or thinly sliced
1 small head Cauliflower, chopped
1 c. chopped Mushrooms
Kosher Salt
Freshly ground Black Pepper
1/4 c. chopped Fresh Parsley
2 tbsp. chopped Fresh Rosemary
1 tbsp. chopped Fresh Sage (or 1 tsp. ground sage)
1/2 c. Vegetable or Chicken Broth

In a large skillet over medium heat, melt butter. Add onion, carrot, and celery and sauté until soft, 7 to 8 minutes. Add cauliflower and mushrooms and season with salt and pepper. Cook until tender, 8 to 10 minutes more. Add parsley, rosemary, and sage and stir until combined, then pour over vegetable broth and cover with a lid. Cover until totally tender and liquid is absorbed, 15 minutes.
Serve.

the comeback
is always stronger
than the set back

Fitspiration

Cinnamon Egg White Pancakes

6 Organic Egg Whites
1 tbsp. Cinnamon
2 packets of Stevia
1 tsp. Alcohol Free Vanilla (whole foods)

Combine all ingredients in a blender and blend on medium for 30-45 seconds. Mixture should be frothy like batter. Heat a skillet and spray olive oil non-stick cooking spray on top. Pour egg white mixture into pan and cook on medium for 1 minute or until top is hard. Flip and cook an additional minute.

Integrity

IS DOING THE RIGHT THING,

EVEN IF NO ONE IS

WATCHING.

INTEGRITY
TRAINING SYSTEMS

Fitspiration

Cinnamon Sweet Squash

1 large Spaghetti Squash roasted and raked
1 tbsp melted Coconut Oil
1 tsp Cinnamon
1 tbsp Kerry Gold butter melted
3 mini scoops of pure Stevia

Add oil, butter, cinnamon and Stevia together. Pour on top of warm squash. Mix well and serve. Tastes great with Salmon or Turkey.

THERE ARE **defeats** more triumphant than *Victories*.

Fitspiration

Fudge Fat Bombs

1 cup Almond Butter
1 cup Coconut Oil
1/2 cup Unsweetened Cocoa Powder
1/3 cup Coconut Flour
1/4 tsp Powdered Stevia or 1-2 tbsp Monk Fruit Sweetener, depending on sweetness preference
1/16 tsp Pink Himalayan Salt

Over medium heat in a small pot, melt and combine almond butter and coconut oil. In the same pot, add dried ingredients and stir until well-combined. Pour mixture into bowl and place in freezer for 40-45 minutes OR pour into silicone mold (if you choose to use a silicone mold, skip steps #4 and #5 and just allow the fat bombs to solidify in freezer, about 2 hours). Once solidified, remove bowl from freezer and form into balls. Tip: regularly wash hands under cold water and wipe with dry paper towel to avoid coconut oil melting in hands. Place formed balls on a flat tray or plate and return to freezer for 15-20 minutes. Eat up!
Store fat bombs in airtight container in the freezer. When you want one, pop one out, allow to thaw for a few minutes, and eat up!

NEVER PUT AN AGE LIMIT
ON YOUR DREAMS...

Fitspiration

Garlic Butter Broccoli

10 cloves Garlic
5 tbsp Olive Oil
3 tbsp Garlic Herb Kerry Gold butter
2 bags frozen Green Giant Chopped Broccoli
2 tsp Sea Salt
1 tsp Pepper
1 dash Frank's Hot Sauce

Microwave both bags of broccoli for 10 minutes. Put your olive oil and whole cloves of garlic in a sauce pan. Simmer on low for 10 to 15 minutes, or until the oil has the garlic fragrance. Set the garlic aside. Pour the oil in a large skillet. Pour the broccoli on top of it. Place the 3 tbsp of butter on top in 3 sections. Cook on medium until cooked to desired doneness. If you like garlic mince it up and add it to the broccoli.
Finish with salt, pepper and a dash of hot sauce. Serves 3 to 10 people.

"Barking is my Cardio"

Fitspiration

Green Bean & Cauliflower Saute

10 cloves Garlic
5 tbsp Olive Oil
1 bag frozen Rice Cauliflower
1 bag frozen Cut Green Beans
2 cups chopped Mushrooms
1 Shallot chopped
3 tbsp Kerry Gold Garlic Butter

2 tsp Sea Salt
1 tsp Pepper
1 tbsp fresh Parsley
2 dashes of Frank's
Hot Sauce

Microwave green beans and cauliflower together for 10 minutes. Saute garlic in olive oil for 10 to 15 minutes or until the garlic fragrance is very apparent. Remove garlic and set aside. Add mushroom and shallot to garlic olive oil. Cook down until soft. Add green beans and cauliflower to the mix and top with the 3 tbsp of garlic butter. Mix well on medium heat until cauliflower starts to turn lightly brown. If you enjoy garlic chop it and add it to the mix. Finish with salt, pepper, parsley and hot sauce and mix well.

CREATE
A LIFE

that feels good
on the inside

NOT ONE THAT
JUST LOOKS

good

ON THE OUTSIDE

Fitspiration

Hearty Hefty Chili

1 Orange Pepper	2 Green Peppers
1 Red Pepper	1 Yellow Pepper
1 Large Onion	1 dash Red Pepper Flakes
3 tbsp Chili Powder	1 dash Cayenne
2 tbsp Onion Powder	1 tbsp Garlic Powder
1 tbsp Sea Salt	2 tbsp Black Pepper
2 tbsp Stevia	1/4 cup Bone Sucking Sauce
6 Stalks of Celery	2 large cans of Tomato Sauce
1 tbsp Franks Hot Sauce	3 lbs. Ground Turkey or Bison

2 cans of Chopped Tomatoes
1/2 small can of Tomato Paste

Chop and saute the veggies in olive oil, cook meat separately and drain. Add all ingredients together. Stir well, cook on medium for 30 minutes. Tastes great served over roasted spaghetti squash.

Trust me, you don't get me want to between and my goals.

Fitspiration

Homemade Italian Tomato Sauce

5 lbs. of fresh Tomatoes
1 small Onion sautéed
2 cloves Garlic, minced & sautéed
1 tbsp Italian seasoning
1 tbsp Oregano
1 tbsp Onion powder

1/2 tsp Red Pepper flakes
2-3 tbsp Stevia in the Raw
3 dash of Franks Hot sauce
1/2 tbsp Black Pepper
2 tsp Salt

Peel and seed the tomatoes (to peel, cut a small "x" on the top and drop in to boiling water for 10 seconds and drop in to an ice bath (Skin will easily peel off). Saute veggies. Combine all ingredients, slow simmer on low heat for 2-3 hours or until cooked down and starting to darken. Use fresh or store in the fridge up to 1 week, or can it according to your canner's instructions for tomato products.

Before

After

Mark Roberts

Before

After

Dave Reynolds

BELIEVE IN YOURSELF.

INTEGRITY
TRAINING SYSTEMS

Fitspiration

Integrity Salad
Kale & Brussels Sprout Salad with Walnuts & Lemon-Mustard Dressing

Salad:

1 Cup Walnuts, chopped

1 pound Brussels Sprouts,

thinly sliced (shredded from Trader Joe's)

1 bunch curly Kale

(remove thick center rib), thinly sliced

1 cup crumbled Feta cheese

For the Dressing:

¼ cup Fresh Lemon Juice

(from about 2 lemons)

½ cup Extra Virgin Olive Oil

1 tbsp Dijon mustard

2 tbsp finely chopped Shallots

1 small clove Garlic, minced

½ tsp Salt

½ tsp Pepper

Preheat the oven to 350°F. Line a baking sheet with aluminum foil for easy clean-up. Bake the walnuts for 5-8 minutes, until toasted and fragrant. Keep a close eye on them; they burn quickly. Combine the brussels sprouts and kale in a large bowl. Make the dressing by combining all of the ingredients in a small bowl. Pour over the vegetables. Add most of the walnuts and cheese, reserving some to garnish the platter, and toss well. Let the salad sit at room temperature for at least 30 minutes (or up to a few hours in the fridge) to allow the flavors to meld and the vegetables to soften. Taste and adjust seasoning if necessary. Transfer to a serving dish and scatter the remaining walnuts and cheese over top. Serve at room temperature.

Recipe provided by Kim Simon

The Battle is Real... The LORD is my Strength

INTEGRITY TRAINING SYSTEMS

Prayer is my Weapon!

Fitspiration

Keto Biscuits

1 cup Almond Flour
1/4 tsp Celtic sea salt
1 tsp Baking Powder
4 Egg Whites
2 TBS VERY COLD Organic Butter (cut into pieces) or cold Coconut Oil
OPTIONS: add 1 tsp of garlic or your favorite spice

Preheat oven to 400 degrees F. Grease a cookie sheet or muffin pan with coconut oil spray. Whip egg whites until very fluffy. In a separate medium bowl, mix the baking powder into the almond flour. Then cut in the butter and salt (if the butter isn't chilled, the biscuits don't turn out). Gently fold in the dry mixture into the whites. Dollop the dough onto the cookie sheet (or muffin tin) and bake for 11-15 minutes. Makes 8 servings.

Credit: Maria Emmerich, www.mariamindbodyhealth.com

"ALL OUR DREAMS CAN COME TRUE, IF WE HAVE THE COURAGE TO PURSUE THEM."

~Walt Disney

INTEGRITY
TRAINING SYSTEMS

Fitspiration

Keto Fudge

1 cup Coconut Oil, soft yet still solid
1/4 cup Full-Fat Coconut Milk
1/4 cup Organic Cocoa Powder
1/4 cup Swerve Sweetener (Confectioners Style)
1 tsp Vanilla Oil or Extract
1/2 tsp Almond Oil Extract
1/2 tsp Celtic Sea Salt
Better Stevia English Toffee to taste
Cinnamon to taste
Pumpkin Spice to taste

Place the coconut oil and coconut milk in a medium-sized bowl and mix with a hand mixer on high for 6 minutes or until well combined and glossy. TIP: I used my stand mixer. Place the remaining ingredients in the bowl and stir on low speed until the cocoa is combined (so it doesn't poof all over your kitchen). Increase speed, and mix until everything is well combined. Taste the fudge and adjust to desired sweetness. Place a sheet of parchment or wax paper along the inside of a loaf pan or divide among a mini muffin silicone mold. Pour fudge into pan or mold. Place the pan or mold in the freezer for at least 15 minutes, until just set. Use the edges of the parchment to pull the fudge out of the pan or pop the fudge out of the mold. Store in an airtight container in the freezer, it will liquefy if you leave it in a warm area. Makes 12 servings.
Recipe submitted by Nicki Bean

SUCCESS HAS NOTHING TO
DO WITH WHAT YOU GAIN IN
LIFE OR ACCOMPLISH FOR
YOURSELF. IT'S WHAT YOU DO
FOR OTHERS.

Keto Zucchini Bread

3/4 cup loosely packed Shredded Zucchini
6 Eggs (4 of them separated)
1/2 cup Coconut Milk (or 2 more eggs)
1/2 cup Coconut Oil (or butter) melted
(plus extra from greasing pan)
1/2 cup Swerve (or Erythritol and 1 tsp stevia glycerite)
1 tsp Pure Vanilla
1 1/2 tsp Cinnamon
1/2 tsp Celtic Sea Salt
3/4 cup Coconut Flour
1 tsp Baking Powder

Preheat oven to 350 degrees. Grease a 9x5x3 inch loaf pan
with coconut oil or butter. Separate 4 eggs into two bowls.
Whip the egg whites until very fluffy. In the other bowl, blend
together the 4 egg yolks, zucchini, oil, coconut milk, sweetener, vanilla, cinnamon, and salt. Then add the other 2 eggs (or
4 if not using coconut milk), one at a time, beating well after
each addition. Combine coconut flour and baking powder and
sift into batter. Blend until there are no lumps. Gently fold in
the egg whites to the batter. Pour
into a greased pan. Top with unsweetened coconut flakes and bake
for 60 minute or until an inserted
toothpick comes out clean. Cool
and enjoy! Makes 14 servings.

Credit: Maria Emmerich,
www.mariamindbodyhealth.com

Fitspiration

Lemon Fat Bombs

7 oz Coconut Butter
1/4 cup Coconut Oil
Lemon Zest from 2 Lemons
15 drops of Stevia

Soften butter and oil, zest lemons. Mix all and pour into candy mold or small glass dish. Cool for about an hour in refrigerator. Keep chilled.

Created by Lisa Klaus-Ogden

The greatest

pleasure in

life is doing

what people

say *you* can

not do.

INTEGRITY
TRAINING SYSTEMS

Fitspiration

Mashed Sweet Potatoes & Cranberry Sauce

Mashed Sweet Potatoes
6 Medium sweet potatoes
Cinnamon
Stevia
1 tbsp Agave Nectar
1 tbsp Unsweetened Almond Milk

Preheat oven to 400°F, Wash sweet potatoes and lay on a cookie sheet. Bake for 90 minutes. Remove from oven and let cool. Peel off the skin and mash the sweet potatoes in a bowl. Add agave nectar, almond milk, and more cinnamon & Stevia to taste. Blend with a hand mixer until smooth.

Cranberry Sauce
2 bags of Cranberries frozen or fresh
1 1/2 cups of Water
1/2 cup of Agave
1/2 cup of Granulated Stevia
1/2 of Juiced Orange

Simmer on medium heat until all the cranberries pop. Keep stirring constantly until your desired thickness. I like to serve mine with toasted walnuts.

WE THEN THAT ARE STRONG OUGHT TO BEAR THE INFIRMITIES OF THE WEAK, AND NOT TO PLEASE OURSELVES.

ROMANS 15:1

Fitspiration

Meatloaf

3 lbs Ground Beef
1 tbsp of Fresh Chives
1 tbsp of Fresh Thyme
1 tbsp of Fresh Parsley
3 whole large Eggs

2/3 cup Unsweetened Almond Milk
1 whole White Onion, chopped
1 cup of Celery, chopped
1/2 tbsp of Olive Oil
1 1/3 cup of Riced Cauliflower, ground to powder

Sauce:
2 cups of Chicken or Beef Stock
10 cloves of Garlic that has been sauteed with onion & celery
3 tbsp. Grass-fed Butter at room temp

Sautee Onion and Celery in Olive Oil.
Combine all meatloaf ingredients into a bowl, reserve some of the spices to garnish once cooked. Line a sheet cake pan with parchment paper and flatten out completely. Shape into a long meatloaf down the center of the pan. Bake for 40-50 mins at 350°. Test at 40 mins, thermometer should read 150°-160° Let rest outside oven to cook more. Combine all sauce ingredients and cook until thickened. Pour over the top of cooked meatloaf. Add extra herbs from meatloaf to the top.

FIGHTIN
for
Change

INTEGRITY
TRAINING + SYSTEMS

Fitspiration

Peanut Butter Protein Cookies

1 cup of Smuckers All Natural Peanut Butter
1/2 cup Baking Stevia
1 whole large Egg
1 tsp Alcohol Free Vanilla
1 tsp Aluminum Free Baking Powder
1 tsp Cinnamon
1 tbsp Vanilla Jay Robb Protein Powder
1 whole mashed Banana
1 tbsp Agave

Combine all ingredients into a large bowl. Mix with whisk or hand mixer until well blended. Use small ice cream scoop to spread evenly distributed cookies across parchment paper or lined cookie sheet. Cook on 350 for 10-12 minutes. Should make 16 bite size cookies.

WITHOUT
AMBITION
ONE STARTS NOTHING.

WITHOUT
WORK
ONE FINISHES
NOTHING.

THE PRIZE
WILL NOT BE
SENT TO YOU.

YOU HAVE TO
WIN IT.

Fitspiration

Power Juice

1 Cucumber
1 handful of Spinach
3 Celery Sticks
3 Asparagus Sticks
1/2 Carrot
1/2 of an Apple
1/2 cup of Fresh Parsley
1 tbsp MCT Oil
1 scoop of Vanilla Jay Robb Egg White protein

Juice all vegetables and fruits fresh. Add to blender with fresh parsley, mct oil & vanilla protein.
This juice is packed with micro-nutrients!

LOOK INSIDE MY SOUL
AND SEE
HOW BAD I WANT IT

Fitspiration

Protein Latte

Makes 12 oz of coffee

1/2 tbsp Coconut Oil or 1 tbsp of Coconut Butter
1/2 tsp raw Cacao Powder
2 scoops Collagen Protein Powder
2 tbsp Unsweetened Coconut Milk
Stevia to taste.

Blend until well blended and enjoy a great way to start the day!

WE
RISE

BY
LIFTING
OTHERS

INTEGRITY
TRAINING SYSTEMS

Fitspiration

Pumpkin Pie

CRUST:
3/4 cup Blanched Almond Flour
1/4 cup Coconut Flour
1/2 cup Coconut Oil or Butter
1/2 cup Just Like Sugar (or Swerve)

1 tsp Stevia Glycerite
1/4 tsp Celtic Sea Salt
1 Egg

FILLING:
1 (15 ounce) can Pumpkin
1 cup Coconut Milk (OR 1 cup Cream Cheese)
1 tsp pure Vanilla or Maple Extract
1/2 tsp ground Cinnamon
1/2 tsp Celtic sea salt
1/4 tsp Ginger
1/4 tsp Nutmeg
3/4 cup Swerve (or Just Like Brown Sugar)
2 tsp Gelatin
1/4 cup hot Water

CRUST: Preheat oven to 325 degrees F. Grease a 9 inch pie pan. In a medium bowl, mix ingredients. NOTE: Just Like Sugar is 96g fiber/cup; do not add to "melted" butter. This will cause it to gel up and get hard. This will be a thick pie dough, press onto bottom of pie pan. Place in oven to pre-bake the crust. Bake for 15 minutes or until lightly golden brown. Remove from oven and set aside to cool.

FILLING: In large mixing bowl, dissolve gelatin in 1/4 cup boiling water. Combine pumpkin, coconut milk, cinnamon, maple flavoring, ginger, nutmeg, Swerve and salt; mix into the gelatin. Pour into pie shell. Cover the edges of the pie with aluminum foil (otherwise it will burn). Bake at 350 degrees F for 70 minutes or until set in the middle. Top with whipped cream or coconut cream and enjoy! Store covered in refrigerator.

Credit: Maria Emmerich,
www.mariamindbodyhealth.com

Recovery from
heart surgery:
Start slow.
One step at a time.
Recovery is a process.
It takes time, it takes patience,
it takes everything you've got.

INTEGRITY
TRAINING + SYSTEMS

Fitspiration

Rana's Vegetable Soup

2 tbsp Olive Oil
1 cup chopped Onion
1 cup thinly sliced Leeks
(whites only)
1 cup thinly sliced Celery
2 tbsp Italian seasoning
2 tbsp Cilantro

1 can (28 oz) diced Tomatoes with juice
(puree with chunks of tomato)
2 1/2 boxes of Vegetable Broth
Organic chicken cube granules
8 cups mixed Veggies
(Green Beans, Carrots, Okra, Zucchini)
1 tbsp Tomato Paste

Heat oil in large stockpot, add onions, leeks, celery and italian seasoning. Cook 58 minutes till onions are translucent. Add broth (2 boxes), tomatoes and their juice, tomato paste and 3 cups water. Bring to a boil. Reduce heat to simmer, cook uncovered (30 mins). Add veggies and return to simmer (I put another 1/2 box stock...dependent on thickness preference. Cook uncovered until veggies are tender about 30-45 mins. Season with salt and pepper to taste, add chicken stock granules to create more depth in taste if needed. I let it cook another 15-30 mins, adjust to your liking.

YOU ARE YOUR ONLY LIMIT.

Fitspiration

Roasted Broccoli

4 lbs. organic Broccoli florets
4 tbsps. Extra-Virgin Olive Oil
4 cloves Garlic, thinly sliced
11/2 tsps. Salt
11/2 tsps. Pepper
2 tsps grated organic Lemon zest
2 tbsps. fresh organic Lemon juice
1 tsp. Onion Powder

Preheat oven to 425°F. Line a sheet cake pan with foil. Spread broccoli in a single layer over the pan and drizzle with olive oil. Sprinkle garlic, salt, pepper and onion powder evenly over broccoli. Roast for 20-25 minutes until crisp and some tips are browned. Immediately add zest, juice and 11/2 tablespoons of olive oil and toss. Oh, this makes broccoli taste like candy!!!

Fitspiration

Roasted Brussels Sprouts

2 - 3 lbs. of fresh Brussels Sprouts (cut in half)
1 large Shallot
1 tbsp Olive Oil
Sea Salt
Pepper
1 tbsp of Onion Powder
2 cloves of Garlic, minced

Saute shallot, garlic and olive oil. Roll fresh Brussels Sprouts in the mixture. Foil line a sheet cake pan, lay veggie mixture out evenly. Bake at 350 for 30 minutes, toss them around and cook 15 minutes more, or until desired doneness.

SET YOUR BAR HIGH, BE KIND, AND DO MORE OF WHAT MAKES YOU STRONGER.

INTEGRITY
TRAINING ✚ SYSTEMS

Fitspiration

Sauteed Cabbage

1 medium Yellow Onion, chopped
2 cloves Garlic, minced or pressed
1 medium head Green Cabbage, sliced into ¾" thick slices
2 Tablespoons Butter, cut into 2 pieces
Salt and pepper to taste
Red pepper flakes, optional

Heat a 12" skillet with olive oil over medium heat. Add the chopped onion and cook until onion is softened, about 3-4 minutes. Add the garlic and stir, cooking an additional 30 seconds. Turn heat up to medium-high heat and add about 1/3 of the cabbage. Stir to mix onions and garlic with the cabbage. Now leave it alone and let the cabbage start to brown, but be careful not to let it burn. Using a spatula, turn the cabbage over and let other side brown slightly. Season lightly with a dash of salt. Add another 1/3 of the cabbage and 1 table-spoon butter. Flip cabbage again after a couple minutes. Finish with remaining cabbage and last tablespoon of butter. Once cabbage is browned to your liking, add more salt to taste and pepper, if desired. Remove from heat, season with red pepper flakes, if desired. Serve.

helmet of salvation

The Ephesians 6:12 Warrior

breastplate of righteousness

shield of faith

always be ready... he is.

Truth

INTEGRITY
TRAINING SYSTEMS

Fitspiration

Strawberry Vinaigrette Dressing

4 cups of Strawberries
1 large Shallot or 1/2 Red Onion
1 tbsp Dried Tarragon
1 tbsp Dried Parsley
1/2 cup Red Wine Vinegar
1/2 cup Water
1/2 cup of Olive Oil
3 heaping tbsp Stevia in the Raw

Put all ingredients above in a blender until desired consistency. Keep refrigerated. Keeps about 2 weeks.

Teamwork IS THE SECRET THAT MAKES COMMON PEOPLE ACHIEVE UNCOMMON *Results.*

Fitspiration

Tangy Coleslaw

4 bags of Coleslaw
1/2 cup of Olive Oil
1/2 cup Apple Cider Vinegar
1/2 cup of Bone Sucking Sauce
1 tbsp. of Franks Hot Sauce
1 tbsp. of Stevia
1 tsp. of Sea Salt
1 tsp. of Pepper
1 tbsp. of Emerill's Horseradish Mustard

Mix all ingredients and let rest in fridge overnight.

OMG...I CAN'T LOSE WEIGHT. IT MUST BE MY TRAINER'S FAULT

Fitspiration

Uncured Bacon, Beef & Mushrooms

6 strips uncured no sugar added bacon
2lbs grass fed beef
2 cups chopped organic mushrooms
1 cup chopped yellow onion
1 cup beef bone broth
2 tbsp garlic herb Kerry Gold butter
2 tbsp Avocado oil
1 tbsp fresh parsley
2 tsp sea salt
1 tsp pepper
1 dash Frank's Hot Sauce

Chop the bacon raw in small pieces. Add bacon, mushrooms, onion and avocado oil to a skillet and cook. Brown the 2lbs of beef. Add to the onion mixture. Add bone broth and butter to a saucepan. Bring to a boil until thickened. Pour over meat and veggie mixture. Let cook on low to medium covered for 5 minutes to combine. Add salt, pepper, hot sauce and parsley. I service on top of a bed of mixed cauliflower or spaghetti squash.

Integrity

is doing the right

thing even when

no one is watching.

C.S. Lewis

Uncured Bacon & Brussels Sprouts

30 Fresh Brussels Sprouts cut in half
1 medium white onion chopped
6 strips no sugar added uncured bacon
5 tbsp Avocado oil
2 tsp salt
1 tsp pepper

Prepare a sheet cake pan. I place parchment paper down first to keep the pan from bringing. Saute onion in 1 tbsp Avocado oil. Chop bacon raw into small pieces. Add Brussels, onion, bacon,oil, salt and pepper into a large bowl. Mix with hands well until well coated. Lay evenly on sheet cake pan. Bake for 40 minutes on 350. Use a spatula to move them around the pan half way through.

Failure is a Bruise not a Tattoo

INTEGRITY
TRAINING † SYSTEMS

Fitspiration

Zesty Pot Roast

2 cups Beef Broth
1 tbsp Lime Zest
3 tbsp Fresh Lime Juice
1 large Chopped Tomatoes
1/4 tsp Cayenne

1 (3lb.) Boneless Chuck Roasts
1 tbsp Kosher Salt
1 tsp Ground Black Pepper
2 tbsp Olive Oil
1 Medium Onion, chopped
1 tsp minced Fresh Garlic

Preheat oven to 350°. Sprinkle roast with salt and pepper. Cook roast in 11/2 tsp hot oil in a dutch oven over medium-high heat 4 minutes on each side. Sauté onion in 1 tbsp hot oil in dutch oven 4 minutes. Add garlic; sauté 1 minute. Return roast to dutch oven; add broth, zest, juice, and tomatoes. Bake, covered, at 350° for 3 hours or until beef is tender. Let roast stand 10 minutes. Slice roast, and serve with 11/2 cups tomato mixture.

Thank you to an amazing staff of trainers. You are champions. God bless you for supporting the vision I have to bless people and save people through health and wellness.

Thanks be to God. You are my reason. You are my why. I serve you in all that I do. May I always live a life that's pleasing to you. Your Grace is sufficient.

I can do all things
through Christ
who strengthens me.

Philippians 4:13

Courage is being afraid & going ahead with the journey anyhow"

-John Wayne

you were the best friend a girl could ask for.

Rest in Peace Fremont
November 13, 2017

Made in the USA
Columbia, SC
25 September 2022

67589836R00046